The Fatherless Wound

A Path to Healing & Reconciliation

Trina D. Payne

Printed in Atlanta, GA

Interior Imaging: Trenise Payne, Chayil Home Solutions – https://chayilhomesolutions.com/

Bookcover Design: Brandon Jolly, Brandon Graphic Designs - https://www.brangraphicd.com/

DFP Agency (Publishing Division)
www.dfpagency.org

Table of Contents

Note to the Reader

Footnotes and references throughout the document will be identified as BIB and can be found in the Bibliography at the back of the book.

***

All scripture references are from the New King James Version of the Bible unless otherwise noted.

Acknowledgements

I am forever grateful to God whose love and guidance helped me to write this book.

A big thank you to my father who was open to sharing with me the circumstances that led to him not being involved in my life. Also, to my mother who did her very best for me and my two brothers, always making sure that we were well cared for as a single mother.

Special thanks to both of my daughters who encouraged me to write this book. We call ourselves the Three T's and we were able to stand strong together when faced with the death of their father, my husband. I appreciate my family and friends who were there encouraging me to write on a topic that was so painful for most of my life.

Thank you so much to my friend Ashley Newell, who prayed and walked with me through my unforgettable experience of meeting my father and her continual support on this journey.

Thanks also to everyone on the publishing team who assisted me every step of the way with writing this book, especially to Deborah Franklin, the ever patient and helpful Publisher; Jackie (JC) Gardner, my meticulous and insightful Editor; Brandon Jolly, the polished and dynamic Cover Designer; and daughter Trenise Payne, who customized the amazing photos for the inside of the book.

Introduction

I have had the pleasure of working in the child welfare field since 2001. The trauma caused by children growing up without their fathers is something that occurs way too often. As a child welfare professional, I am concerned about the safety, permanence, and well-being of children who touch in any way the child welfare system. It should be noted that this book is also being written from the perspective of someone who grew up with her father being absent from her life and not meeting him until she was an adult.

Despite challenges and setbacks, I realized that God was always there and cared about me. Over time, I was able to depend on God for strength and have experienced His healing power in several areas of my life, including the wound caused by being fatherless.

Children growing up fatherless is an epidemic that can impact them in many ways. This wound can also affect their children, and potentially, even their legacy can be forever altered. As a society, we must be willing to look at the ugly truth about this problem and do something about it. My sincere desire is to help children and adults who are living without their fathers to find a path to healing and, if possible, reconciliation.

As an African American woman, I am aware that the phenomenon of children growing up fatherless goes back to slavery. Think about it: men were often used simply as breeders. In addition, enslaved children were constantly separated from their parents and forced to grow up in kinship families. As a result, they did not receive the love they needed from their biological parents.

Fathers had to watch their women being raped by the master and there was nothing he could do to help her. So many enslaved children were born into this world with the master being their father. One example of how this historical trauma has been passed down through time is the way some African American families have struggled with openly expressing affection and validation to their children. During slavery, the fathers who were also the plantation masters—often denied their own mixed-race children to maintain their social and economic power. This rejection left deep wounds, creating a generational cycle of emotional distance, survival-based parenting, and difficulty in forming secure attachments.

In some families, this manifests as a reluctance to verbally affirm children with phrases like "I love you" or to offer physical affection, not because love isn't present, but because generations before had to suppress such expressions to survive. While many families have worked to heal these cycles, the echo of this historical pain still influences parenting styles, emotional availability, and the way love is communicated across generations.

Chapter 1:
What Does It Mean to Have
A Fatherless Wound?

Life is a journey and not a one-time event. As we go through life, it is expected that we know and have a relationship with our family. Along the way, we will experience feelings of love, joy, and pain, and many of these moments are intimately connected to our families. For some of us, we have not met our fathers or had contact with them for quite some time. The impact of our father not being around can cause a Fatherless Wound.

To have a Fatherless Wound means to walk through life as if we can only identify with half of who we are. It's the weirdest thing to feel like there's a blank slate concerning who you are, where you came from, and the BIG question of *whether you will ever meet or reconnect with your father?* It is the grief that comes from wanting to feel our father's love, yet it is not present. It is a deep desire, a yearning to be loved by him.

The Fatherless Wound

When we go through life with a Fatherless Wound, it is traumatic and can cause us to be emotionally distressed. Everyone experiences this trauma in different ways, such as feelings of abandonment, low self-esteem, and depression, because they are living life without their father's love. Some people have turned to drugs, alcohol, risky sexual activities, unhealthy relationships, or other destructive behaviors to numb the pain of fatherlessness (BIB A). Other fatherless children have left their homes and are now homeless or have become victims of sex trafficking. You may also experience strong feelings of loss because your father's presence is missing in your life. As a result, you walk around with an open wound that continues to bleed out.

As a teenager and then later as an adult, I found myself walking through life full of pain, like something was missing, because I could only identify with my maternal side. I kept it a secret for so long, hoping that no one would ask me about my father. Only some of my closest friends even knew that I had never met him. Reflecting on that, I realized that not many people were talking a lot about their fathers. That caused me to wonder if they also had a Fatherless Wound and did not want to talk about it as well. I would always cringe inside when participating in conversations where I knew that I might have to say something about my father. It got even harder for me when my daughter started asking about her maternal grandfather, and I had nothing to tell her -- no specific details, no pictures, no information about where he might be or how to contact him. The memory is still very fresh from when she was in elementary school and was asked to make a family tree. She needed a photo of her grandfather, and I had nothing to give her. It was heart-wrenching to see yet another generation in pain, all because I could not tell her if her grandfather was dead or alive or provide any other facts about him.

While there isn't a specific statistic quantifying the exact percentage of Americans experiencing a "father wound," data indicates that father absence is a significant issue in the United States. According to the U.S. Census Bureau, over 17 million children, or more than one in four, live without a father in the home (BIB B). Additionally, the National Fatherhood Initiative reports that when a child grows up in a father-absent home, they are more likely to suffer emotional and behavioral problems (BIB C). This data highlights the widespread nature of father absence and its potential impact on individuals and families across the nation.

Chapter 2:
Where Are the Fathers?

The Fatherless Wound

The "Present" Father

Some fathers are physically present but emotionally absent. In other words, the father does not have a meaningful relationship with the child. Although he may have surface-level conversations in the home with the child, he does not express his love with his words, hugs, or kisses. Showing affection is a real challenge for the present father as it is hard to give something when he did not have this experience himself. It can be a difficult thing for the father to love his child and not be comfortable with expressing his love. Love is a language that needs to be heard, felt, and can be experienced in so many ways, but it needs to have the freedom of expression.

Just imagine you are growing up and your father is living in the home or is involved in your life. You see him on a regular basis, but when it comes to him checking in to see how you are doing or sharing about his life, there is just not much he has to say. He has not learned how to be open and willing to express himself in a positive and healthy manner. As a result, you are void of having a loving and trusting relationship with your father.

Where Are the Fathers?

Have you ever asked the question, "What is it about your father that makes him so distant even though he is physically present?" He may very well be repeating the same pattern of communication as his father, growing up in a home where he was seen but not actually being raised by his father. The only way for him to change is to first acknowledge that his behavior is not healthy and is negatively impacting his child.

Society has also played a part in the way fathers view their role. They receive messages like fathers are supposed to be strong, work hard, take care of their family, and are not to show positive emotions. Not much, though, about how to express love by saying and doing kind and thoughtful things or showing other emotions like compassion, adoration, appreciation, calmness, forgiveness and joy. It is likely that they may be more comfortable with negative emotions like sadness, anger, disgust, anxiety, fear and disappointment.

The truth is that most fathers did not have a blueprint on how to be an effective parent who was loving and nurturing; instead, they wounded the child. The examples they followed were not always the most appropriate role models. They simply learned from their own father, or if their father was not involved, they watched other fathers who were in their friend circle or community.

The Deceased Father

Did you know that you can go into adulthood still feeling the pain from the loss of your deceased father? Or your father may have died while you were an adult, and you continue to experience feelings of pain from the loss. Whether your father died of natural causes, medical complications, violence, or other reasons, unaddressed grief is very real. If you don't allow yourself to go through the stages of grief, you will be stuck, still feeling the pain from no longer having a father you can communicate with or connect to in any way. If your father was not involved in your life, unfortunately, you are now unable to talk with him and reconcile your relationship. Going through the stages of grief and loss that will be discussed later in the book is critical to your being healed.

Where Are the Fathers?

The Unknown Father

If you are the child of an unknown father, you have blanks in your life that need to be filled in with answered questions. Have you ever asked your mother or family these questions?

- Who is my father?
- Where does he live?
- Do you know how I can reach him or his family?

These are just some of the questions that may come up in your life if the identity of your father or his whereabouts are unknown. It is very possible that if he lives in your general area, you have seen him or a paternal family member at some point. What if you have passed his home or been in his neighborhood and didn't even know that you were so close yet so far away at the same time?

If you have decided to find your father, many resources are available today, i.e., social media, various internet searches, private investigators, and companies such as Ancestry.com that will help you to identify family members. You may eventually meet him, and he is everything you have dreamed about. Or he may be going through things in his own life or have had past experiences that may not fit what you hoped for in a father. Either way, you did not get to choose who your biological father would be. It is important that you first determine *why* you want to find your father. Once you locate him, this will help you not to have unrealistic expectations and be open to loving and accepting him no matter his circumstances.

The Divorced Father

When the mother and father decide they no longer want to be married, the child will be directly impacted by this decision. After a divorce, couples often experience consequences from the separation, which could include decreased levels of happiness because divorce is a loss. Loss can be interpreted as a change in economic status, emotional distress, loneliness, depression, and so on. Many children find it difficult to cope with their parents getting divorced. The effects can include academic, behavioral, and psychological problems; therefore, the parents should consider the child's needs as they plan for their care and well-being (BIB D).

Where Are the Fathers?

The degree of hostility and amount of conflict between parents influences how they will grow up. It is not uncommon for the children to remain with the mother having full custody; therefore, a father may no longer be present in the child's life or spend as much time as he did once he is divorced and out of the home. Having positive communication with the mother is critical so they can co-parent effectively. The child now must adjust to this change and needs reassurance from both parents that they love and are there for the child.

It is both parents' responsibility to continue making efforts for the father to be involved in the child's life. Fathers who desire to have full or joint custody by the court will need to learn how to file for custody in their state and determine their visitation rights. Choosing not to see the child because these matters are not resolved is no excuse and could cause valuable time to be lost that could have been spent with the child.

The Abusive Father

A child is abused when they are harmed physically, mentally, emotionally, or sexually. Factors to consider for fathers who abuse their children include their being under the influence of drugs or alcohol, having difficulty managing stress and anger, relationship problems, and domestic violence. Some warning signs of potential abuse are threats to harm you, following or chasing you with the intent to abuse you, and having weapons, including any kind of harmful objects, in his presence.

There are times when it is necessary for the mother to make the decision to keep the father away from the child to protect herself, the child, or both of them from his abuse. Even as an adult, depending on the circumstances, you may need to maintain a distance from him for a while to make sure you are safe. It is also possible that legal action must be taken by filing a civil protection order, restraining order, etc., to ensure your safety. You should also create a safety plan with details on who to contact and how to escape in case an incident is about to occur, where to go, and what important papers and personal items to have close by in case you need to leave immediately.

Where Are the Fathers?

It is possible that your father may have also been abused and is repeating the same behaviors that he learned. If you were abused by your father, you are missing out on having a healthy relationship with him. No matter whether the abuse was physical, mental, emotional, or sexual, it is not your fault that you were abused. Having an abusive father can cause harm and continue to show up as an adult if this issue is left unaddressed. Some of the effects of abuse include emotional dysregulation, depression and mood disorders, lack of self-confidence, poor self-esteem, behavior problems, and challenges with social interactions.

The Forced Absentee Father

What exactly is a forced absentee father? This is seen when the father has a desire to be involved, but he cannot due to obstacles in the way of his maintaining a relationship with the child. One reason why the forced absentee father is not involved in the child's life is baby-mama drama. Sadly, the relationship challenges between the mother and father have resulted in the child being used as a pawn. The mother may choose to keep the father away from the child out of spite because she is feeling hurt from the breakup with him. Consequently, the child pays the ultimate price because they will miss out on having a relationship with the father.

There are situations when the father is not able to communicate with the child because the in-laws have created roadblocks when they do not feel he is a good influence or have other concerns about him. Other reasons are when fathers work long hours, live/work out of the local area, are in the military, have substance abuse, or physical or mental health issues. In some cases, it is possible for the father to have virtual or phone contact, even though he is faced with the challenge of not seeing the child in person.

The Imprisoned Father

A child with a father in prison may find themselves asking, "When is he coming home?" Once he is released, you may wonder if he will stay home for good this time. Being in a locked facility means that a father is unable to make his own personal choices daily. He is told when to get up and go to bed and what to eat, and he has restricted activities as well as visiting hours.

Regardless of the reason why the father is in prison, it is important to provide an age-appropriate explanation to the child on why he is in prison, the duration, and the plan to connect with him. However, some children are prevented from seeing their father based on the decision of their mother or other caregiver. This could be based on a desire to protect them, a perspective that prison is no place for a child, or other reasons. Therefore, the mother or caregiver will not encourage visits, letters, or any other means of communication.

In some instances, the father chooses not to have the child visit him in prison. He may feel ashamed and embarrassed for his actions and being in a restrained environment where he has lost his personal freedom. The father's decision not to have visits can significantly impact the child. Unless there are extenuating circumstances, it is in the best interest of the child to have ongoing contact with the father.

Some fathers who are in prison have been able to develop a positive relationship with their children. This requires the father to be very intentional in his communication with the child. He must be focused to prevent being distracted by prison life. The efforts of fathers who maintain contact with their children despite being in prison are valuable. Whether they have in-person visits, write letters, or talk on the phone, it makes a difference in the development of their child. Thankfully, there are organizations whose mission is to make sure that children can make connections and build healthy relationships with their fathers.

The Wrong Father

Were you told that one man is your father, only to discover later that another man is your biological father? Perhaps your mother or other family thought they were being helpful by protecting you from your father. Some mothers decide to lie about who the daddy really is because of their own infidelity with their husband or significant other. Either way, you were misinformed and have a right to know the truth about your father. Award-winning gospel artist Kirk Franklin announced to the public in September 2023 that the man he thought was his father was the wrong father. He was openly shocked by this new discovery and found out when he had not one, but two DNA tests. Unfortunately for Kirk, his mother was not able to tell him the truth about his father, even after he had the DNA tests.

No child should ever have to discover that they grew up with the wrong father. It can make you feel like you have been robbed of having a true relationship with the right father because all your energy was put towards the wrong father. Now you must deal with all the memories you have, good or bad, with someone who was based on a false sense of what was real.

The Financially Distant and Non-Custodial Father

It is interesting how a father's lack of involvement in their child's life can be due to whether they are paying child support. This could be through a court or an informal arrangement for him to provide financially for the child. A father should willingly give money to make sure his child's needs are met. In addition to the money, the child still needs the father's time, love, and attention, and these other needs do not have a price tag attached to them.

But if he feels inadequate because he is not financially providing for the care of his child, this may cause him to not be around.

Fathers of Children in the Child Welfare System

Some of the children receiving services from the child welfare system are growing up without their fathers. Their trauma usually includes feelings of separation, loss, and abandonment. These children may experience behavioral challenges in the home, school, and community, and several foster care placement disruptions. They could also be a part of other service systems (i.e., juvenile justice, mental health, and care for human trafficking victims).

In many instances, the fathers of these children are not involved in case planning. It typically takes several efforts by the caseworker to build rapport with the father. This is extremely helpful in getting his buy-in to be on board with case planning and achieving the agreed-upon goals.

Other fathers in the system have not been identified, or their whereabouts are unknown. Caseworkers have been able to locate them by reaching out to family and friends, researching historical records, and for some, through databases to see if the father's name is known. There are men who choose to act in the role of a father for the child, and others who believe they are the father, but the paternity has yet to be confirmed in court. These fathers may or may not be involved in their life.

It is all too common for a child in the child welfare system to not be connected with their father or have a healthy relationship with him. One child, Johnny, comes to mind. When I met Johnny, he was eight years old and did not know his father's name or anything about him. Unfortunately, his mother was not a reliable source of information about his father, and there was no way to search for him.

What really caught my attention with Johnny was that he had a difficult time trying to understand why he did not know his father and asked as many questions as possible about him. It was truly heart-wrenching to watch Johnny try to make sense of a problem that was so much bigger than he could fully understand. Fortunately, he was supported by people who were affectionate towards him and willing to listen and answer his questions as often as needed. He also had an amazing therapist who was able to work well with him. Although this remained a pain point for Johnny, he was able to cope better.

Chapter 3:

Little Susie's Story

The Fatherless Wound

I grew up without knowing my father. As a child, the only unconditional love that I experienced from a fatherly figure was from my brother's grandfather. He considered me his own granddaughter and nicknamed me Little Susie. There are tears in my eyes as I write about him because we had a close bond. Granddaddy had a special place in my heart throughout my life, even now that he has passed.

As a child and well into my adult years, I was walking through life with a Fatherless Wound, full of pain, like something was missing. It was like walking around and knowing that I came from a mother and father but only being able to identify with one side -- my maternal family. The paternal side of me was void and grayed out. Most people were not aware that I did not know my father. It's not that I lied, it just was not discussed in conversations. It was as if most kids around me just knew that we don't talk about our fathers, and many were also fatherless.

My mother is one of ten children, so growing up there were always a lot of family around and big holiday gatherings. But still, even with all the connections with my maternal family, it did not take away from the longing to know my father. I would find myself wondering, *what did he look like? Is he looking for me, or did he forget about me? Is he still alive? Does he live in the area?* One of the biggest questions I had was, what if I walked past him and didn't even know he was my father? These questions kept leading me to want to find him. There'd be times back in the day when I would look through the phone book and then write up a list of everyone with his name. As time went on, I would do internet searches as well. Usually, I would get overwhelmed by the number of people with the same name. My search would then stop because I would get distracted by life's circumstances. At one point, I even considered hiring a private investigator or a company that could find your loved one.

God delivered me from the Fatherless Wound at a women's conference in September 2017. I was on my way down to the altar for a group prayer. The conference host, Pastor Minoli Haththotuwa of Open Heaven Church, stopped in front of me and looked me right in the face. As I was looking at her eyes, they seemed to exude God's love deeply. I began to experience the weightiness of God's presence as He spoke prophetically through the pastor. He let me know I am His daughter, and He loves me. No more will I be sad about my parents' love. I am His daughter. He informed me that I had been feeling bitter towards my mother, which I did not realize until that very moment. You see, I was so focused on not knowing my father or having his love that I was not paying attention to feeling bitter because my mother could not give me information on how to find him. She just did not know where he was.

Although I was walking around as an adult with these thoughts, the little girl who was wounded deeply was crying out inside and yearning for a connection with her father. But God knew just how much this gaping hole in my heart was hurting me. During this encounter, God also said that when I look in the mirror, I should see Jesus's reflection. On this day, I was visited by Heaven.

I am very grateful that Father God delivered me. Since that time, I have been healed from the pain of not knowing my father. Later, Father God let me know the pain was due to a

Fatherless Wound. I had no idea, but I was happy about no longer having to experience this pain. Receiving Father God in my heart has been life changing. The level of intimacy in my relationship with Him has grown significantly. For some people, it may sound strange for me to talk about having a relationship with God. But this is a relationship in which I need to feel whole, and it has proven to be beneficial as He continues to order my steps and take care of me.

The truth is that many people find it difficult to acknowledge, respect, honor, and follow God's principles and guidance because of the relationship they have with their own father. The relationship between a child with a Fatherless Wound and their father is often a contentious one. If their father is wounded due to his connection with his father, it will spill over into the relationship you have with him. The reason is because this issue is left unresolved. It is critical that your father can address what happened to him and be restored from this wound. Only then will he have the strength to love you the way you need to be loved. Every child who is experiencing a Fatherless Wound needs to be healed and walk their own path to restoration and hopefully reconciliation with their father.

Years later, in 2021, I realized that even though I was healed from the pain of not knowing my father and his lack of involvement in my life, the same question came up again. What if I walk past him and don't even know it's my father? By this time, my expectations were simple. All I wanted to know was whether my father was still alive and see his face so that I could at least identify him and not pass by him on the street.

With hope and determination, I started to search for him again. As I was doing an internet search, this time was different because there were photos of some of the men. There was one photo that I saw which made me ponder. His facial structure reminded me of my own, even though we did not look exactly alike. Another thing was that there was an address listed for him. So, I did what any girl who is longing to know her father would do and took another step. I wrote a letter to him with information that only he would know about and went to his home with my husband and daughter.

My plan was to introduce myself to him, but if he was not home, I would leave the letter. There were a lot of emotions leading up to and on that day. I have seen many of those television shows where people meet their loved ones for the first time, and you just don't know how things can turn out. I had thoughts like, *what if he couldn't care less about ever meeting me?* For this reason, I kept my expectations low about how he would receive me, but it was something I had to do.

A few days later, after leaving the letter, I noticed a missed call that went to my voicemail. When checking the message, **I was blown away to hear him introduce himself to me and ask me to give him a call.** Pulling myself together as best as possible, I called my father for the very first time. He told me he had left a couple of messages on my phone, but somehow, I had overlooked them with all the busyness of that week. I almost fainted when we were talking for the very first time. Both of us were very emotionally raw, and it was a lot to take in and process. We agreed to talk again. I can only vaguely remember our conversations early on because they were so emotionally charged for both of us, trying to catch up on the past and update each other on our current lives. What I do remember is that meeting him was amazing, awesome, and a truly unforgettable experience.

I am grateful for taking this step to find my father. We are continuing to get to know each other. Remember, my only expectation was to know if he was alive and how he looked. I never thought about anything beyond that, as far as actually having a relationship with him.

We are taking things one step at a time and continuing to grow and build our relationship. My father made it very clear from day one how grateful he was to know me and that he loved me. Most of the time, when we ended our phone calls or departed from each other, he'd give me encouraging words, which I absolutely loved, and they seemed to reach a place inside of me that belonged only to him. I had my first conversation with my father on the phone on October 1, 2021. By this time, I was already whole and in a relationship with Father God.

I had a chance to talk with my father about why he was not involved in my life. He told me that when I was born, he was not ready to be in a committed relationship with my mother. During that time, my father was running the streets and thought he knew it all. Over the years, he tried to look for my mother, but she had already moved, and he could not find her.

Many fathers repeat the same cycle as their own father, who was not a part of their lives. In my father's case, he did not have his father in his life growing up, nor did he have any positive male figures. He was raised by his maternal grandmother in a neighborhood close to where my mother grew up. His family told him his father was killed in the war. It amazes me how families keep secrets because they think it is best to protect you rather than just tell you the truth about your father. When he was sixteen years old, he was shocked when his father showed up at his home and was sitting in the living room. My father got angry and wanted nothing to do with him. He had to work through his feelings of hurt, anger, and unforgiveness. It took a while for him to open his heart and be willing to communicate with his father. Eventually, they were able to form a good relationship.

The Fatherless Wound

When writing this book, I asked my father what his biggest regret was. He told me that not being there for me was his biggest regret, and he felt the worst thing was knowing that he did not do his best to support me. I asked him what he would like to say to anyone who does not know their father. His response was not to give up. He also said that your original father is God. He had to realize that his own father was just a man. Man will let you down, but not God. Man does not have all the answers. It may seem at times that God won't answer you, but the answer may be in front of you all the time. There could also be something that was said to you, but you may have shunned it because you were not ready to believe it. When we leave each other or just when we are about to get off the phone, he always tells me, "God be with you. I love you. I appreciate you, and God bless you." I have come to realize that there is no one else who could say these words to me, where they resonate so deeply inside of me, but my father.

What is interesting is that there are seventy-seven days between my father's birthday and the first time we talked on the phone. That same year, I turned 52, which is the year my father was born - 1952. He turned 69 that year, which is the year I was born - 1969. I was curious about what these numbers meant and learned that in Biblical numerology, 7 symbolizes completion or perfection (BIB E). The number 77 is found in the Bible in Matthew chapter 18 and verse 22, where Jesus is responding to a question about how many times to forgive. He tells his disciple, Peter, that he should forgive 77 times to demonstrate the importance of forgiveness. I truly believe that the way these dates came together is more than a coincidence, but we were divinely at the right time to meet.

Now that I have met my biological father, I call him dad and continue to have a relationship with Father God and see Him as my Father first and foremost. Although there was no way to choose who my biological mother and father would be or whether they would be able to raise me, one thing that is for sure is that I am not a mistake. It was God's plan for me to be born, and He has a purpose for my life. Jeremiah chapter 29:11 says...*I know the thoughts that I think toward you, saith the LORD, thoughts of peace, and not of evil, to give you a future and a hope.*

Chapter 4:
The Father's Love

Love is a universal word that everyone has the right to experience. It is felt that no matter our race, color, religion, sex, national origin, disability, age, etc. Love shows up in our five senses. We can feel love based on what a person says and how they touch us. Love can be seen by what someone does for us. It can be heard in the tone in the way someone speaks to us. When we smell a person's body scent, fragrance, or perfume, it can evoke an emotion in us towards them. Some have also experienced love in the way something tastes, for example, someone gives you a meal or something sweet you really enjoyed. This chapter will look at the father's love from the perspective of a biological and biblical father.

Your Biological Father's Love

Children deserve to have a bond with their father. Without it, they feel like something in them is broken. They also have trouble figuring out who they are and where they fit in the world. Having a bond is necessary for them to feel complete, accepted, protected, and loved. The father is meant to be a model to them on how to make their way and be a contributing member of society. They are left with the media and other influences to tell them what to expect and show them how to become an adult and parent to their own children.

Research has shown that a father's love is just as important as—or sometimes even more important than—a mother's love. Unfortunately, some men believe they are not supposed to show their emotions, which can affect their relationships with their children and others. When they were growing up, their fathers might not have even been around very much. However, fatherless fathers, or dads whose fathers showed them very little love, are not doomed to repeat their childhood experiences (BIB F).

Fathers who enjoy a loving, nurturing relationship with their children have important opportunities to influence the direction they take in life. Studies have demonstrated that young people whose fathers are actively involved in their lives have greater self-confidence, perform better in school, and are better able to avoid risky behaviors. But being a loving father is not an easy task. It requires additional commitment and extra time, no matter what your children's age. Fathers must learn about the different stages of child development and become familiar with the strengths, weaknesses, personalities, and specific needs of their children as individuals (BIB G).

Father God's Love

Imagine being caught in a raging storm at sea—waves crashing, wind howling, darkness all around. You're lost, unsure which way to go. Then, in the distance, a light appears. A lighthouse, steady and unmoved, guiding you safely to shore. That light doesn't ask where you've been, what mistakes you've made, or whether you fully understand its purpose—it simply shines, offering direction, security, and hope.

Many describe God's love in this way. It is constant, unwavering, and available to all, whether you recognize it immediately or not. Some call it Father God's love, while others see it as an unseen force of grace that meets them in their darkest moments. No matter what name we give it, love has a way of finding us, especially when we need it most. This metaphor makes everyone feel included and shows God's love in a way that both those who already believe and those still figuring things out can relate to.

The Father's Love

It's important to note that for me, faith plays an integral part in my daily life. This may not apply to everyone reading this book, but I would be remiss not to share how my faith walk allowed me to have many breakthroughs while on the journey of feeling empty because I did not have my father in my life. In addition, of all the ways God could have chosen to relate to humanity, He chose the language of family. He could have described Himself as a benevolent dictator, a kind boss, or a patient landlord. But instead, He chose the word Father.

He presents Himself as a Father because we all have an idea of what a father is and does. Even if we did not have earthly fathers who treated us well, we have a fundamental understanding of what a good father should be. God planted that understanding in our hearts. We all have a need to feel cared for, cherished, safe, and valued. Ideally, an earthly father will meet those needs. But even if he doesn't, Father God will. Jesus taught His followers to address God as Father (Luke 11:2). Throughout scripture, God describes His love for us as that of a caring parent (Isaiah 49:15; John 16:26–27; 2 Corinthians 6:18). Although He possesses characteristics of both Father and Mother (Isaiah 66:13), He chooses the masculine word because it also denotes strength, protection, and provision (Psalm 54:4).

The Fatherless Wound

God has a special place in His heart for the orphans and fatherless (Deuteronomy 24:20; Jeremiah 49:11; James 1:27). "Though my father and mother forsake me, the LORD will receive me." Psalm 27:10 (NIV) God knows that many times earthly fathers have been absent or have not done their job (Ephesians 6:4). He offers to fill the role of a Father (John 6:37; Deuteronomy 1:31). He invites us to call out to Him when we are in trouble (Psalm 50:15), to cast all our worries on Him (1 Peter 5:7), and to enjoy His company (1 Corinthians 1:9: Psalm 116:1; 1 John 5:14). He models for us the characteristics He had in mind when He designed fatherhood. Although many times earthly fathers do not live up to the ideal, God promises that, in Him, no one has to be without a perfect Father (BIB H).

Unfortunately, many people find it difficult to relate to Father God because of the issues they have with their own father. They ask how can God love and be there for me if my own father is not in my life? This is very real for so many people. Just because people believe that there is a God does not necessarily mean that they are open to His love or desire to be a Father to the fatherless (Psalm 68:5). Think about it. If you have no bond with your own father, or the bond has been broken, then there is no model for having a relationship with Father God. Having a relationship with God means spending time to get to know Him. Through the scriptures in the Bible, I can understand His perspective on so many issues and how He feels about us.

In my experience, having a relationship with Father God has been a source of tremendous help. When I am distracted and focused on so many things, I am reminded that He loves me and is with me. There are times when life is pulling this way and that way with all its busyness. During those times, I didn't feel as close to God and had to put a lot more effort into figuring things out. Those times are like walking in a dark room and trying to find the light switch. But, when I take the time to praise and worship God through music, prayer, declarations, and in conversations, I sense His presence and love and receive revelation and direction for my life much quicker. 1 Corinthians Chapter 13 talks more about love and how it never fails. It points out how you can have possessions and be doing so many things, but without love, you gain nothing. Two of my favorite songs about the love of God are "Reckless

The Fatherless Wound

Love of God" by Cory Asbury and "I Can Only Imagine" by
MercyMe.

The Bible has a lot to say about Father God. Below are a
few scriptures that reassure me of His love:

- *... O LORD, You have searched me and known me.--*
  Psalm 139:1

- *...the love with which You loved Me may be in them, and I
  in them. --* John 17:26

- *The LORD is near to those who have a broken heart, and
  saves such as have a contrite spirit. --* Psalm 34:18

- *Your eyes saw my substance, being yet unformed. And in your
  book they all were written, The days fashioned for me,
  When as yet there were none of them.... --*Psalm 139: 16

- *And we have known and believed the love that God has for
  us. God is love, and he who abides in love abides in God, and
  God in him. --*1 John 4:16

- *For I am persuaded that neither death nor life, nor angels
  nor principalities nor powers, nor things present nor things to
  come, nor height nor depth, nor any other created thing, shall
  be able to separate us from the love of God which is in Christ
  Jesus our Lord. --*Romans 8:38-39

The Father's Love

When I think of being loved by a father, the first thing I think about is Father God's love for me. He was the only reference I had to having a father until I found my biological father. My relationship with Father God has grown and intensified over time based on my understanding of what His love means.

God's love is all-encompassing. My research (BIB I) has shown that there are four types of love He has established:

1. **Agape Love:** In Greek, which is the primary language of the New Testament, *agape* love is considered the highest form of love.

   Agape love is all about loving someone no matter what. It does not matter what the person has said or previously done; this kind of love is expressed to others without expecting anything in return. It's the kind of love that puts others first and doesn't come with strings attached. It gives everything to someone else. You choose to love, even when you don't have to—that's what makes it so powerful.

The Fatherless Wound

See Bible verses below related to Agape Love of God

- *"But God demonstrates His own love toward us, in that while we were still sinners, Christ died for us."*—Romans 5:8

- *"By this we know love because He laid down His life for us. And we also ought to lay down our lives for the brethren."*— 1 John 3:16

- *"Beloved, let us love one another, for love is of God; and everyone who loves is born of God and knows God. He who does not love does not know God, for God is love. In this the love of God was manifested toward us, that God has sent His only begotten Son into the world, that we might live through Him. In this is love, not that we loved God, but that He loved us and sent His Son to be the propitiation for our sins."*—1 John 4:7-10

2. Storge Love: Storge is a Greek word for love that describes the natural affection found within families—between parents and children, siblings, and even spouses. This kind of love usually develops as relationships grow over time. It's steadfast, devoted, shields others from harm, and strong enough to weather life's challenges. Even though the word *storge* doesn't appear in Scripture, there are plenty of verses that show God's intentional plan for familial love.

It should be noted that the opposite of storge is *astorgos*. This is a term found in the Bible that means "without natural affection." In Romans 1:31 and 2 Timothy 3:3, Paul warns that in the end times, people will become so selfish that even the love found between family members will be absent.

See Bible verses below related to Storge Love of God

- *Husbands, love your wives, just as Christ also loved the church and gave Himself for her, that He might sanctify and cleanse her with the washing of water by the word…"*—Ephesians 5:25-26

- *"Children, obey your parents in the Lord, for this is right. 'Honor your father and mother,' which is the first commandment with promise: 'that it may be well with you and you may live long on the earth.'"*—Ephesians 6:1-3

- *"Love suffers long and is kind; love does not envy; love does not parade itself, is not puffed up; does not behave rudely, does not seek its own, is not provoked, thinks no evil; does not rejoice in iniquity, but rejoices in the truth; bears all things, believes all things, hopes all things, endures all things. Love never fails. But whether there are prophecies, they will fail; whether there are tongues, they will cease; whether there is knowledge, it will vanish away.*"—1 Corinthians 13:4-8

3. Phileo Love: In the Bible, *phileo* is the word used for the kind of love between close friends. It's the kind of relationship where you consider your friends as family and are bonded by this connection.

In Romans 12:10, Paul tells us to love each other with real affection and to enjoy putting others before ourselves. The Greek word he uses is *Philadelphia*, which means brotherly love. We're encouraged to treat our friends, neighbors, and everyone else with the same kind of love and care we would give to family.

See Bible verses below related to Phileo Love of God

- *"Greater love has no one than this, than to lay down one's life for his friends."*—John 15:13
- *"A new commandment I give to you, that you love one another; as I have loved you, that you also love one another. By this all will know that you are My disciples, if you have love for one another."*—John 13:34-35

- *"Beloved, let us love one another, for love is of God; and everyone who loves is born of God and knows God. He who does not love does not know God, for God is love."*—1 John 4:7

4. Eros Love: Eros love is the kind of love that describes the romantic and sexual connection between a husband and wife. The Bible gives a beautiful example of it in the Song of Solomon, where a married couple is deeply in love, drawn to each other, and deeply bonded.

This kind of love gives us a glimpse of how God intended for passion and closeness to look in marriage. Unfortunately, it has been turned into something it was never meant to be—confusing, oversexualized, and far from God's plan. But eros love was designed by God to be something special, shared between husband and wife in marriage, with their relationship built on Christ. It's meant to be celebrated within the safe and loving boundaries of marriage.

See Bible verses below related to Eros Love of God

- *"Let him kiss me with the kisses of his mouth—for your love is better than wine. Because of the fragrance of your good ointments, your name is ointment poured forth; therefore, the virgins love you. Draw me away!"*—Song of Solomon 1:2–4

- *"Marriage is honorable among all, and the bed undefiled; but fornicators and adulterers God will judge."*—Hebrews 13:4

- *"But I say to the unmarried and to the widows: It is good for them if they remain even as I am; but if they cannot exercise self-control, let them marry. For it is better to marry than to burn with passion."*—1 Corinthians 7:8-9

Final Thoughts: Consider how the truth about God's love and these verses make you think and feel. Does it cause you to see God's love in another way compared to before? Perhaps you have observed that God's love can be interpreted as both simple and deep at the same time.

For many people, God's love is a difficult topic based on what they were told and perhaps their own experiences. You could be unsure about accepting God's love. You might feel like you don't deserve it or think you need to earn it. But the truth is, all you need to do is **receive it**. God's love opens the way to an understanding of what love really is.

The Father's Love

God is love, and there is no other love like it. His love is deep, pure, and completely selfless. Here is an example in John 3:16 of how Jesus shows us what that love looks like: *"For God so loved the world that He gave His only begotten Son, that whoever believes in Him should not perish but have everlasting life."*

You can't even begin to grasp how big God's love for you truly is. 1 John 4:7-8 says that God is love—whether it's agape, storge, phileo, or eros—it covers everything. His love is ever-present and deeply protective. You just have to trust in His love.

The angel of the Lord encamps all around those who fear Him and delivers them. Oh, taste and see that the Lord is good; blessed is the man who trusts in Him! – Psalm 34:7-8

Chapter 5:
On the Other Side

The Fatherless Wound

There is hope for the wounded and a path to healing and reconciliation. You do not have to continue going through life weighed down, frustrated, or even angry because of the pain caused by not having a father. You can change the way you feel about your father, whether he is currently involved in your life or not. For some, this will be uncharted territory. It will require you to be open and willing to do something different to have a better relationship with your father.

If you don't know where your father is and you are feeling the void of a Fatherless Wound, continue to search for him. You may want to consider seeking assistance from a locator service or investigator to do the work for you. Even if your father has died, you have the right to have peace in your heart and closure when it comes to the connection you had with him. If you have a father who was abusive, I recommend that you seek help to heal from this trauma and then determine if it is safe for you to reconcile with him. Although it is possible to have a healthy relationship with him, making sure you remain safe and seeking support and guidance along the way is important. No matter the circumstances that led you to this point, there is hope.

Below are some things to consider as well as resources that are available for you on this journey to healing and reconciliation.

Father Figures

The need for father figures is great. As a society, many children are being raised by single mothers. Even though a child does not have a biological father in their life, they can still benefit greatly by having a father figure who can provide nurturance and meet their needs. Every child who is growing up without a biological father in their life should have the opportunity to build a healthy relationship with a father figure. Stephen Kendrick of the Kendrick Brothers (well-known film producers and creators of a documentary on fatherhood) outlines seven roles that a father plays in the life of his family: provider, protector, leader, teacher, helper, encourager, and friend (BIB J). A father figure can play one or more of these roles for the child. The guidance and support that they provide to a child will impact their development and make a positive difference in their life.

The Fatherless Wound

A father figure plays a vital role in a child's emotional, social, and cognitive development. Whether he is a biological father, stepfather, grandfather, mentor, or another supportive male presence, a father figure offers guidance, protection, and encouragement. He models responsibility, resilience, and empathy, helping children learn how to navigate life's challenges with confidence and self-control. Research shows that children with involved father figures are more likely to perform well academically, develop healthy self-esteem, and avoid risky behaviors. For example, a report from the U.S. Department of Health and Human Services found that father involvement is associated with better outcomes in school performance and emotional well-being, as well as reduced likelihood of substance abuse and criminal activity. Beyond discipline or authority, a father figure fosters emotional security and stability, contributing to a child's overall well-being and future success (BIB K).

Some examples of father figures include:

- Godfathers
- Grandfathers

- Other Male Family Members
- Family Friends
- Mentors (i.e., spiritual & professional mentors)
- Foster & Adoptive Fathers
- School Teachers
- Sports Coaches

Ask Yourself:

- Who was in the role of a father figure in your life?
- How did their support and guidance have an impact on you?
- For females, is there a father figure you can connect with a child?
- For males, is there a child you can help by being his/her father figure?

Top Tips for Father Figures:

Children look up to positive male role models in their life. As a man, you can play a unique role in another child's life.

1. Be Positive and Intentional with Your Communication.

Intentionally make your interactions with nephews, nieces, or your children's friends a source of encouragement. Recognize that your attitude towards them will make the difference in the quality of your interactions. Taking the time to listen to what they have to say in a non-judgmental way will help you develop an open and trusting relationship.

2. Seek Out Other Father Figures for Your Own Children.
It's always good for your child to have other positive male role models in their life. This will allow them to learn and be mentored by other healthy and well-rounded men. Your child will also gain more insight into the unique experiences they have with the father figures, which can leave a lasting impression on their lives.

3. Be a Role Model.
Children look up to positive male role models, each having a different impact on girls and boys. Take a minute to think about how life was when you grew up and what you felt was missing. This could be the very thing you could provide for a child to make things better for them. If you have a desire to give guidance to a child, be intentional and trust that opportunities will present themselves to be a role model.

4. Take Other Children Along with Your Own Children.

Take part in activities together like football, camping, dinner, or movies. As a father figure, by taking a child along with your children, you can help them feel included and help to expand their sense of family. In addition, when your children's friends come along during family activities, this is a great way to get to know them and be ready to offer support when needed.

5. Where Possible, Provide Encouragement to Sole-Parent (Single Parent) Mothers.

Encourage them to consider appropriate father figures for their children. Single mothers usually need additional help because they are busy working and/or may have little to no help with their child. You can help them recognize the benefits of their child having a father figure and, if possible, assist with identifying the right person (BIB L).

So many single mothers are taking on the role of trying to be the child's mother and father. This is a daunting task that they were never supposed to face. After all, what should a mother tell their child when that child looks them in the face and they can see the pain in the child's eyes, knowing that the child is wondering where their father is? Why has he not come to see me, or what have I done to make him not want me? These are questions that so many mothers are dealing with. Or perhaps they should take the other option, which is not to say anything to the child and simply refuse to talk about the father's whereabouts. This may seem like the easiest route to take, but it still won't answer the child's questions and certainly won't resolve this issue.

Have you ever heard the saying, "It takes a village to raise a child"? This is very true. It is so important that the child can be connected to a good role model. This will allow the child to receive guidance and support from someone who is positive and supportive, and although not a replacement for their father, can still provide love.

So, I encourage single mothers to be willing, although painful, to get help and the support that they need. You do not have to go alone. Taking on this load all by yourself is an added stress and something that you simply do not have to do. Make sure that you have a good support system--one or more people in your corner that you feel comfortable talking with or even connecting with a therapist or a peer who has been where you are now, who can provide guidance to you. God did not intend for you to have to deal with this on your own, and you are certainly not on an island all by yourself; there are others who can help you.

A Path to Healing

Most children who grow up without their father at some point in their lives feel that he abandoned them. Merriam-Webster's Dictionary defines *abandoned* as left without needed protection, care, or support. This means that you never met your father, or he is no longer involved in your life. Over time, the pain from abandonment can fester and show up in other ways, such as seeing yourself as unlovable, emotionally unavailable, and unworthy. It can lead to being overachievers, pleasure seekers, trying to fix our partners, and hurting people who hurt others.

Being abandoned can also cause people to feel rejected. According to Merriam-Webster's Dictionary, to be *rejected* means someone is not wanted, unsatisfactory, or does not fulfill requirements. These feelings can make you believe that you are not valuable and cause you to have a desire to want to be accepted by others. This is a flat-out lie. The truth is that each one of us is here on this earth with a purpose and is very valuable. As a fatherless child who has experienced abandonment and/or rejection, you deserve to be loved and feel safe and secure.

In Kirk Franklin's documentary, he shared how he found his real biological father. He talked about the pain that he had felt over the years from not knowing his father and his challenges with finding out the truth from his mother. His testimony opened the door for many people to talk about their own Fatherless Wound experience (BIB M).

Grief and Loss

When a father has died or is not involved for other reasons, the child can experience feelings of grief and loss. Grief is a natural response to loss and can be seen in various stages such as shock or denial, anger, bargaining, depression, and acceptance. There is no guarantee how a person will react to grief, and it is critical to have a support system to help you address these feelings. Because everyone is different, some people will not experience all the stages of grief. For many, grief may not show up in the same way or in the same order. It can cause changes in your daily life, such as your appetite, sleep, mood, energy, and has been known to affect a person's health. The more you understand about grief and loss, the better you will be able to cope. If you had a relationship with your father, you now have an opportunity to treasure the good memories, teachable moments, and address any hurtful memories.

Therapy

Whether intentional or not, the effects of rejection in childhood may include fear of intimacy, distrust, anxiety, depression, and people-pleasing behaviors. Feelings of confusion and emotional pain from rejection may lead to attachment challenges, ineffective coping mechanisms, or an overall sense of loneliness.

While you can heal from rejection in childhood (or adulthood) by creating new, nurturing experiences, a mental health professional can be a valuable resource for working through the more challenging effects of rejection. Healing is possible, and support is available (BIB N).

Traditional therapy and spiritual guidance/counseling are both healing paths that people have used to overcome Fatherless Wounds. For me, the path included recognizing and being open to Father God's love. I have benefited tremendously as a child of God from this relationship and know that I am complete, accepted, secure, and loved by Him. This reassures me that no matter what happens in life, Father God will always be with me.

In fact, everyone needs to have a way to work through all the built-up thoughts and feelings and the actions caused by the pain of not having your father involved in your life. Your path to healing should be specific to your individual needs. The most important thing is to recognize that you do not have to live as a wounded person and can get help to rise above this challenge.

Chapter 6:
A Path to Reconciliation

The Fatherless Wound

For the Wounded

If you have ever considered what it would be like to reconnect with your father, it is possible to have a healthy relationship with him. Anyone who has a father who has died can benefit from counseling support to help them work through their loss. It is important to express the type of relationship you wanted with your father. You can work through your feelings about how life was growing up without him. This applies even if he died when you were an adult. Know that it is never too late to forgive him.

For children who grew up with their fathers kept away from them -- whether it was by their mother or because he was in prison-- there is hope for you. The circumstances that led to your father being kept from you do not have to keep you from him. You can change the trajectory of the relationship with him by pressing RESET. Begin now to reach out to him and talk about the reason he was not involved in your life growing up and let him know you would like to start fresh. He may be too scared or just not know how to take the first step.

Ask Yourself:

- How do you communicate with your father now, or when he was involved in the past?
- If connected with your father now, are you comfortable expressing your feelings?
- Is there anything you would change about the way you communicate with him?

You can seek the help of someone neutral. Perhaps a therapist or someone you know who can be objective and help you work through your feelings as you move forward towards reconciliation. The reality is that your father is who he is and may not measure up to your expectations or give you what you feel you need from him. I encourage you to keep an open mind and heart and have much success as you journey on the path to healing and reconciliation!

For the Fathers

For fathers who were kept away from their child, don't give up on trying to work things out with the child's mother. Realize that the mother is probably hurt by something you said or did, and this is what is driving her decision to keep you from your child. When she is barreling insults and hurtful things towards you, I encourage you to find a way to turn the situation around and get to a place where you can improve your relationship with her. You may need to involve a therapist or someone who can be objective to facilitate communication between the two of you for a while.

It is important to allow the mother to have her voice heard and know that you are listening intently to what she has to say. Be remorseful and ask for forgiveness for the role you played in the relationship coming to an end. Check yourself to see if you are feeling offended because of how she has behaved. Be determined to work through these issues and develop a new relationship with the mother. Hopefully, things will change over time if you focus on what is best for the child.

Strengthening your relationship with your children begins with you, but you don't have to do it alone. Considering someone you admire as a role model can be a valuable first step. Invite this person to mentor you as you work to repair and grow your bond with your children. Ask for practical advice and tips that can help you become the loving father you aspire to be. There are also books, videos, and online resources regarding fatherhood that you can access to support and encourage you on this journey.

As mentioned, seek to work with a therapist who is a good fit to support you. Start building a more loving connection with your children by responding to several important needs.

- **Children need an involved father.** Simply spend time with your children. Pay attention to them, together and individually, and share conversations. Talking about their favorite television shows, music, friends, school activities, and other interests is a good start. Involved fathers often make sacrifices, such as giving up some of their own favorite activities, to devote more time to interacting with their children. Together, make memories your children will keep for a lifetime.

- **Children need an accepting father.** Make your children understand that you love them for who they are *rather than for what they do*. Although you will hold them accountable for their decisions and behaviors, you will love them no matter what. Teenagers who feel accepted by their fathers are more likely to trust them and open up about their thoughts, fears, and dreams.

- **Children need an affectionate father.** Fathers can show affection in a variety of ways. Tell your children often that you love them. Gentle, encouraging words or a simple hug, especially when they are not expected, can strengthen family relationships tremendously compared to the actual effort they took. When a father shows affection to his children, they understand they are loved and worthy of that love.

- **Children need a consistent father.** When fathers maintain steady parenting habits, children know what to expect and what is expected of them. Constant support, fair rules, and regular enforcement give children certainty in their lives, helping them grow and thrive. Fathers should aim to show their children consistent behavior, even when it is difficult to do so.

- **Children need an available father.** A father who is routinely unavailable to his children or teenagers, despite saying he loves them, can make them believe that other aspects of his life take priority. When a dad is available, he proves to his children that they are important. Being available can be as simple as clearing the dinner table with a young child, helping a middle schooler with homework, or chatting with a high school student's friend (BIB O).

Many fathers have indeed decided to be a part of their child's life. Perhaps it's because you remember that you also grew up without a father and that it was challenging. Now you have decided to make a difference and step up and be a father to your own child. I applaud you because this certainly cannot be easy. You may be thinking, *I have never had a father who was there as a role model to support me.* I encourage you to find support and others who have been where you are. There are fatherhood support groups, mentors, and men in your circle who can provide you with guidance and support.

As a father, you can work out co-parenting arrangements with the mother so that you are able to participate in the rearing of the child as well as spend time with them. This may not be an easy task, depending on the relationship you have with the mother. It is very possible to work things out and commit to what's most important, which is that your child is raised in an environment where the parents are respectful towards one another. This will also allow you to be available not just physically, but also emotionally and financially to meet the needs of the child.

TIPS & BEST PRACTICES

- **Make a visitation schedule that works for your family.** Are you divorced or separated? Do you only see your kids on weekends? This can be one of the greatest challenges you face as a father. Give your children the time to adjust and make them feel at home. If you have new living arrangements, provide them with their own separate space/room if possible.

- **Become involved in all aspects of your child's life.** The presence of both parents is important for a child's development. Fathers are doing much more hands-on caregiving – i.e., changing diapers, getting up with the child at night, reading books, telling stories, taking the child to the doctor, sharing drop-offs and pick-ups, and helping with homework.

Chapter 7:
Fatherhood & Father Engagement Reimagined

I have noticed that when people know a man is not taking on his responsibilities as a father, he can be treated negatively. While this may seem appropriate for some, especially because they see him as a "no good father", this is in no way helpful to him. In fact, it can place a stigma on him. He, too, could internalize the negative thoughts and feelings that others have about him and then see himself as a "no good father." Enough is enough!

We should cancel viewing fathers in this way. Cancel disrespecting them and not valuing them as a father. Also, cancel not embracing fathers and supporting them. Fathers have a voice; they need the freedom to speak and be heard. Let us not shut them down with our own negative views and judgment towards them. We have no idea what the circumstances are that led a father to a point where he was not involved with his child, although I did present several examples in this book. Therefore, if we are not directly assisting him, we should be in the background cheering for him. Instead of making him feel guilty and ashamed, we can let him know that we are available to support him.

I believe that there is a connection from the past with our ancestors to the present-day father, no matter the race. The way we view fathers needs to change. However, it will require us to understand how we got to this point. If we look back at history, we can learn from how fathers were viewed and the value that was placed on this role. Many fathers were raised that children should be seen but not heard. Whatever ways fathers in the past treated their children can be playing out, even now. In addition, many of our forefathers throughout the generations have experienced pain from traumas they have experienced that have been carried down from one generation to the next.

It is very possible that you may not know why you think or behave in a certain way. You may also notice that many of the fathers in your bloodline seem to have the same issues – i.e., mental illness, substance abuse, domestic violence, inability to express feelings, lack of commitment in relationships, etc., and this is something that was not addressed. As a result, these issues remain unresolved and show up in the way fathers function in society and treat their own children.

There needs to be a shift in how we view this role and a commitment to embrace the father. We must encourage and empower him to step into the role of fatherhood. This may require him to be educated in what it means to be a father and how to parent a child. Take a moment to imagine what it would be like if, on a local, state, and national level, we provided the father with the right support, and if necessary, services that he needs. Hopefully, as a result, more fathers would embrace fatherhood. I have seen fathers treated unfairly in my personal life, and no good has come out of it. But I believe things can change. We need to recognize that continuing to do the same thing in the same way is insanity. Reimagining fatherhood will require all of us to shift our thinking and behavior towards fathers. It is critical that we examine what type of resources they need and how to make sure they get them. There should be more initiatives involving child welfare agencies and community programs collaborating together to strategize on ways to improve fatherhood and father engagement outcomes, research, and development for best practices. In addition, prevention, intervention, and postvention are all necessary to make a significant impact on reimagining how we view and respond to fathers.

In conclusion, reconciliation is not only a means to connect a child with their biological father but can also be for anyone who has had difficulty building a relationship with Father God. God would love to be in your life. According to Ephesians Chapter 2:1-9, it says… *For we are God's handiwork, created in Christ Jesus to do good works, which God prepared in advance for us to do.* (NIV)

Chapter 8:
Self-Care Recommendations

Taking care of yourself is not a pastime but a necessity, especially when you've experienced the hurt of a father not being there. For children who grow up without the connection, support, or affirmation of a father, the emotional impact can be deep. This is the reason why self-care is so important. It's more than pampering yourself; it's about truly caring for your inner self by creating space to process, grow, and restore. In this section, we'll walk through practical and meaningful ways to care for yourself as you move through the pain and begin to heal.

Step 1: Believe You Can Be Healed

Only when we grasp the incredible capacity we have for growing and transforming, healing, and forgiving, can we truly make the most of our lives. Regardless of what it looks or feels like, we can choose how we see our reality. It's a radical level of power and responsibility over one's life when we believe we can be healed. No matter the trauma we experience, we have the right to walk in wholeness.

Step 2: Seek Help

We can't go it alone, not if we really want to reach our true potential. Assistance from a healing professional is not a sign of weakness. Quite the opposite. Letting someone in for the sake of empowering our highest self speaks volumes about our desire-- our willingness to take responsibility for our lives and for our courage to be vulnerable.

Step 3: Become Self-aware

When we understand the emotional impact and behavioral tendencies from having an absent parent or living in a divorced home, we can start to choose proactively how to respond to the pain we experience and respond with greater self-love, control, and wisdom. Otherwise, we live reactively, shooting in the dark by behaving unconsciously, not really knowing what hole we are trying to fill.

For example, most children of an absent and/or divorced parent struggle with two common issues: Fear of abandonment and feeling unworthy of love. These deep wounds tend to bleed into relationships in four harmful ways:

1. People Pleasing - settling for less out of fear of rejection.
2. Needy for love - a desperate latching on to any attention to cover a fear of being alone.
3. Fixing our partner - maybe we could get the love we need if we can fix his/her problems.
4. Emotionally unavailable - never letting people in, hard to commit, and afraid to be vulnerable.

Identifying our behavioral traits leads to the beginning of transforming them. We cannot change what we cannot see, and we also minimize the risk of repeating the cycle.

Step 4: Don't Look Externally to Fill the Void

We need to have a good relationship with ourselves to be whole. As hard and counterintuitive as it may be, we must restrict the urge to have a romantic partner to fill our lack. It's a paradox. The more we work on being good with ourselves,

85

the greater our chances of attracting what we are really looking for. We are people who need people, but it's about timing and priority. We must put our relationship with our true self first. Only then are we truly prepared to attract a soulmate, someone with whom we experience genuine love and belonging that lasts! Likewise, I notice that when I am trusting in God, I do not have to go it alone because my reliance is on His direction.

Step 5: Choose Wisely

Be selective with whom you date, let in, and especially marry. Realize your worth and guard your inner light. Stay away from those who show signs of caring only for themselves, not a family player. Be cautious about taking morsels of attention to assuage your fear of being alone. Break the chain and select someone who appears to be capable and has balance -- who is open to growing and becoming a better person. You are worth it.

Self-Care Recommendations

Step 6: Forgive, Let Go, and Trust

Blame is a heavy first stone on our backs upon which those larger stones of anger, fear, guilt, and shame build. Blaming our parents, and especially blaming ourselves, keeps us stuck and limits our capacity to enjoy the blessings we are meant to receive. We often cannot see the big picture in life; it can be hard to make sense of our losses and hardships. But those who trust the process of life and learn to embrace challenges as opportunities to grow stronger, wiser, and more capable of love, tend to rise higher than those who can't let go and continue to blame. It's not easy to forgive and be compassionate with ourselves. Yet, when we focus on the blessings that we have gained through the pain, and the light revealed from the darkness, we stop wishing for things to be different and appreciate who we are and all that we are given (BIB P).

In addition, if you know someone who is experiencing a Fatherless Wound, you can provide encouragement and resources. Or if you are a fatherless child, consider seeking prayer and other support to help you overcome your wounds.

Bibliography

Chapter 1:
BIB A: A Father's impact on Child Development - Delaware Fatherhood and Family Coalition (March 27, 2024) https://calendar-dffcdads.org/fathers-impact-on-child-development/

BIB B: Living arrangements of children under 18 years old: 1960 to present - U.S. Census Bureau (2023) https://www.fatherhood.org/father-absence-statistic

BIB C: The Father Absence Crisis in America - National Fatherhood Initiative (November 10, 2021) https://www.fatherhood.org/championing-fatherhood/the-father-absence-crisis-infographic

Chapter 2:
BIB D: The Responsibilities of the Noncustodial Parent - Family Education https://www.familyeducation.com/family-life/divorce/custody-child-support/responsibilities-noncustodial-parent

Chapter 3:
BIB E: The Number 7 in the Bible - Bible Study Tools https://www.biblestudytools.com/topical-verses/the-number-7-in-the-bible/

Chapter 4:
BIB F: Unbreakable Bond: The Strength of a Father's Love –
National Responsible Fatherhood Clearinghouse (2008)
https://www.fatherhood.gov/research-and-
resources/unbreakable-bond-strength-fathers-love

BIB G: Unbreakable Bond: The Strength of a Father's Love –
National Responsible Fatherhood Clearinghouse (2008)
https://www.fatherhood.gov/research-and-
resources/unbreakable-bond-strength-fathers-love

BIB H: What does it mean that God is father to the fatherless? -
Got Questions Ministries
https://www.gotquestions.org/father-to-the-fatherless.html

BIB I: What Are Four Types of God's Love – Abundant Life Church.
https://livingproof.co/may-the-love-of-god-surround-
you/#:~:text=First%20John%204%3A7%2D8,fear%20Him%2
C%20and%20delivers%20them.]

Chapter 5:
BIB J: 7 Roles of a Father by Stephen Kendrick – Fatherhood
CoMission
https://www.fatherhoodcomission.com/author/stephen-
kendrick/

BIB K: The Importance of Fathers in the Healthy Development
of Children by Jeffrey Rosenberg and W. Bradford Wilcox - U.S.
Department of Health and Human Services, Administration for
Children and Families (2006) https://cantasd.acf.hhs.gov/wp-
content/uploads/Importance-of-Fathers-Healthy-
Development.pdf

BIB L: Dad-proof Tips: Being a Father Figure - The Fathering Project (September 2022)
https://thefatheringproject.org/fathering-channel/dad-proof-tips-being-a-father-figure/

BIB M: Kirk Franklin's official YouTube video – Father's Day - https://www.youtube.com/watch?v=49SCqvyZM7Q

BIB N: 54 Possible Effects of Physical and Emotional Rejection in Childhood by Hope Gillette - PsychCentral Let's Recap Section (August 18, 2022)
https://psychcentral.com/lib/effects-childhood-rejection#recap

Chapter 6:
BIB O: Unbreakable Bond: The Strength of a Father's Love – National Responsible Fatherhood Clearinghouse (2008)
https://www.fatherhood.gov/research-and-resources/unbreakable-bond-strength-fathers-love

Chapter 7:
BIB P: Hope for Healing the Wound of an Absent Father or Divorce by Dr. Rachel Glik (March 2, 2016)
https://www.drrachelglik.com/blog-posts/2016/3/2/hope-for-healing-the-wound-of-an-absent-father]

About the Author

Trina has worked in the child welfare field for 23 years. She cares deeply about the care and protection of children and youth who grow up in foster care and those who have experienced human trafficking. She is a strong advocate who has spent most of her career working in residential licensing, contract monitoring, and quality assurance to ensure that children and youth's needs are met.

Trina began training and consulting after recognizing that nonprofits and businesses could benefit from having help to build a strong infrastructure, improve management operations, and to better support their employees' well-being. As a lifelong learner, Trina is always looking for ways to enhance her spiritual development, skills, and mindset. She is a mother of four children and enjoys traveling and spending time with family and friends.

For more information or to inquire about Trina speaking at your next event go to:

Website: www.thefatherlesswoundbook.com

Email: admin@trinapayne.com